This Book Belongs To

_____

INTRODUCTION

Have you ever imagined a life, but for some reason, you need a refresher or inspiration to kick things into gear? You have the right journal roadmap. This productivity journal is like no other. It provides 14 days of activities to jump start some important activities simplified to have fun everyday and enough to take action. Understanding how to properly use your journal while we go through our busy lives each day. Let's chart each day with a purpose through properly journaling.

Journal contains an understanding of important learnings explaining the true purpose of journaling, a daily planner, a powerful daily challenge, quotes, journal pages to write freely.

Definitely not a blank lines journal but a workbook to practice and start journaling the write way. Let's have fun!

Take time to do what makes your soul happy

Date:_____

I am grateful for:

7:00 AM	
8:00	**GOALS**
9:00	
10:00	
11:00	
12:00 PM	
1:00	
2:00	
3:00	
4:00	**TO DO**
5:00	
6:00	
7:00	
8:00	
9:00	
10:00	

breakfast	lunch	dinner

NOTES

water ○ ○ ○ ○ ○ ○ ○ ○

exercise

MENTAL CLUTTER

Today we kick-start the 14 days challenge, and one key aspect of journaling is to reduce mental clutter. Our brains are wired to store countless information for retrieval. Like physical clutter make our spaces feel like carrying excess baggage, and is demotivating, mental clutter is anything that makes our minds feel like they're on overdrive. It's the thoughts we have while we're awake that's crucial to daily living, we need what we need now and we're not always wired with patience.

Have you ever experienced walking into a room, and forgetting what exactly you went for? If the answer is yes, don't worry, it happens to the best of us. While you would like to know now what you went for, your brain is working hard, trying to reorganize, defragment, and sieving through clutter to send the signals needed.

If we knew exactly how everything is indexed and stored, we may have a better chance in managing the, "I need to get back to this thought", or "let me recall that long list", or trying to store every password and log in information in our heads for retrieval.

Do you also wonder why someone you know seem to recall things so well, or seems to be somewhat more intellectual at certain topics? Don't beat up yourselves, it all depends on how much information we are depending on our brain to store. **Let's get into a short burst of science.**

The Atkinson–Shiffrin model of memory (Atkinson 1968) suggests that the items stored in short-term memory moves to long-term memory through repeated practice and use. Long-term storage may be similar to learning—the process by which information that may be needed again is stored for recall on demand.

The hippocampus is a critical gateway to long-term storage for memories. If the hippocampus is damaged, you may have trouble recalling details and events from the past. Recall – During this stage, your brain reconstructs the memory from smaller stored pieces. When you remember something, it isn't an exact replay of the experience.

An important aspect of information that's critical for managing our everyday living; is our account numbers that can make or break our long-term goals. Let's lighten the work on our hippocampus and learn to journal a key piece of information your brain is trying to keep in long-term memory.

Minimize **Mental Clutter** To Maximize **Productivity**

DAY 1

Make a list of all account numbers from all institutions. Institutions including banks, mortgage houses, tax and revenue centres, schools, insurance, workplace, company registrars. Do not include loan accounts. Let's put things into perspective. I know this may be the last thing you would want to journal but let's shake things up a bit to start.

Account Name	Institution	Number	Current Status	Resource / Other useful info

Quote of the day: A manager is not a person who can do the work better than his men; he is a person who can get his men to do the work better than he can. **Frederick W. Smith**.

Date:_____

I am grateful for:

Time		GOALS
7:00 AM		
8:00		
9:00		
10:00		
11:00		
12:00 PM		
1:00		
2:00		
3:00		TO DO
4:00		
5:00		
6:00		
7:00		
8:00		
9:00		
10:00		

breakfast	lunch	dinner

NOTES

water ○ ○ ○ ○ ○ ○ ○ ○

exercise

EATING THE "FROG FIRST"

Prior to our day 1 challenge we touched on the topic of mental clutter. Anxiety is fear characterized by behavioural disturbances. Anxiety is not always related to an underlying condition. It may be caused by: stress that can result from work, school, personal relationships, emotional trauma, financial concerns, and stress caused by a chronic or serious medical condition, a major event or performance, side effect of certain medications, alcohol consumption, "ghosting" / social blocking, lack of oxygen.

In some cases, people can be generally anxious without really knowing why. **Normally, the brain manages our fear and anxiety without allowing them to interfere with our daily functioning.** If there's a nearby threat, different areas of the brain help us make sense of the threat by amplifying or quelling our anxiety and fear.

Major factors contributing to high levels of financial anxiety and stress include a lack of assets and insufficient income, high debt, money management challenges and low financial literacy. Women, young adults, people with financially dependent children, and those who are low-income, relationship challenges and underutilized purposes and potentials are mostly financially anxious.

Today, we journal with the intention of "Eating The Frog First". It's almost hard to journal on other topics, when we have the topic of financial statement balances that we have been procrastinating. Today, spend some time, do some checks and research. Proceed to your day 2 challenge

DAY 2

Take control of your debts. This stage is normally scary especially when you have multiple debts, but facing the real status gives you so much power to bring it into control. Let's list them.

Debt / Bank Loan Title	Current Balance	Monthly Payment	Interest / APR	Good or Bad status

Quote "And to preserve their independence, we must not let our rulers load us with perpetual debt.

Date:_____

I am grateful for:

7:00AM	
8:00	
9:00	**GOALS**
10:00	
11:00	
12:00PM	
1:00	
2:00	
3:00	
4:00	**TO DO**
5:00	
6:00	
7:00	
8:00	
9:00	
10:00	

breakfast	lunch	dinner

NOTES

water ○ ○ ○ ○ ○ ○ ○ ○

exercise

MANIFESTATION

How strongly do you believe in the phrase, "All things are possible, to him who believes" – Mark 9:23? Faith and believing in your self is an important ingredient of manifestation.

Manifestation is an indication of the existence, reality, or presence of something. Manifestation is bringing the things you focus on to your physical reality through thoughts, feelings, and beliefs. Manifestation can be an intimidating concept. One tends to not believe possibility until it happens. Today, I want to tell you, "The journey of receiving, starts with creating a place in your mindset to accept".

Essentially, it's a journal you create in order to clarify your vision for your brand, business, passion projects, and life. It helps you set intentions and keep track of your goals so you can break them down into daily action steps. To give you a personal experience I had before I bought my first car. I was a bit fearful in taking the first step; the goal seemed a bit far reaching but I stumbled upon the book; "Purpose Driven Life". I remembered understanding that, in order to attract this, I had to start visualizing the car parked in my garage. It gets better! Let me break the story here a bit and proceed to my first experience of vision board.

Many years ago, I can recall my 10 year's old self. I remember holding on to this beautiful book in which I would write everything that was beautiful to me, new, and anything I saw that I would love to be a part of my life. Even if it was just to take space in my thoughts. Fast track 5 years later at 15 years old in high school; at the start of each year, I would cut things from magazine that I loved. These included; my career look, things that demonstrated my favourite colour well; and most of all, any pictures that showed me what other countries looked like. I loved the idea of travelling. Fast track to age 25 I continued to make these beautiful collages in my book. At age 25, I decided to use a chart on a wall. I started to create the life I wanted using pictures. I remembered one day, watching a YouTube video and was listening to Oprah describing vision board. My mouth dropped, there was this big awakening in my life; because it's the first time I knew the process I was doing was called "vision boarding". I sat down and I could relate to everything she said and took it as a confirmation to always bring thoughts to life. This is one way to declutter your brain but an even more important aspect when we bring it to life on paper.

I may not have manifested everything I still need to, but he limits I placed on myself in manifesting many of my realities today, was because I believed.

DAY 3

Dream a little. Post pictures of your financial goals. Go through magazines, google, newspapers and identify with any photo that represents a financial goal you have. You can post pictures of money in the bank, beautiful home, business, dream car, travels, etc.

"You cannot depend on your eyes when your imagination is out of focus."

Date:_____

I am grateful for:

7:00 AM
8:00
9:00
10:00
11:00
12:00 PM
1:00
2:00
3:00
4:00
5:00
6:00
7:00
8:00
9:00
10:00

GOALS

TO DO

breakfast	lunch	dinner

NOTES

water ◯ ◯ ◯ ◯ ◯ ◯ ◯ ◯

exercise

CIRCLE OF INFLUENCE

Today, if you have heard it 1000 times and it has become a cliché, then I am going to say it 1001 times and tell you to love this cliché if you want to reach your goals. "You're the average of the five people you spend the most time with," a quote attributed most often to motivational speaker Jim Rohn. There's also the "show me your friends and I'll show you your future" derivative. Whichever you've heard, the intent is the same.

Audit the people around you and while we are at it; let's audit ourselves and ensure we are living our purpose of uplifting and building too. To share my learnings from, Jan Johnston Osburn, who is an organizational consultant and certified executive coach, she sums it up in these categories:

The driver brings the dream to reality. They understand the big picture, but they have the talent to break it down into actionable steps. They are results-oriented and are usually decisive, direct and pragmatic. They may fall to the practical side, but they know how to get things done and thrive on the thrill of the challenge.

We need a **motivator** in our circle: This is your voice of inspiration. They keep pushing you to meet your goals. They help you understand that goals are met more frequently when they are tied to a "higher purpose." This person infuses you with energy and enthusiasm.

Your **supporter** is a true friend. This is the person with whom you can let your guard down. They are your comfort zone. They are your safe haven. Comfort is not all that bad at times; just remember that you still have to reach for more. This person will be there with you as you journey through life and they will journey with you. They are excited when you realize success and support you in times of need.

The **devil's** advocate. Yes! This person is the critical thinker. They ask questions and lots of them. They see problems before they arise. This person is crucial because you need their perspective. They won't sugar coat it. They're blunt, but they try to look out for you. You may not always like what they have to say, but they are often the voice of reason.

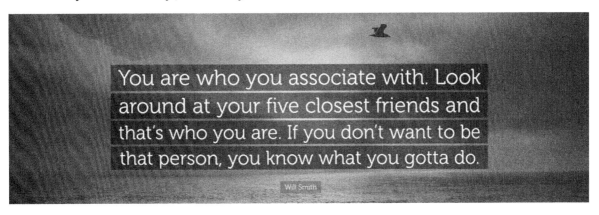

You are who you associate with. Look around at your five closest friends and that's who you are. If you don't want to be that person, you know what you gotta do.

Will Smith

Take the time to look at the type of friends we are and where we would land; inside or out of the circle of influence. While we learn and build, Keith Ferrazzi, in the book "Never Eat Alone" reminds us if we reach out to the people who understand our dreams and goals; and is willing to share and support, we can grow.

DAY 4

Create a people circle of influence and success. Successful people are always willing to share and give. They do not hoard information and they are always great teachers. Today's activity is to identify 10 persons who you are proud of and you would like to emulate. People you list can be anywhere in the world. You must be able to contact each person to have a conversation and discuss your goals.

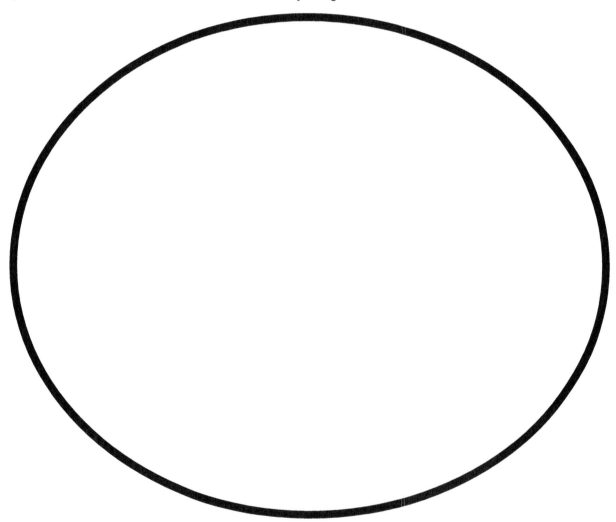

Quote: Attitude is greatly shaped by influence and association. Jim Rohn.

Date:_____

I am grateful for:

7:00 AM		GOALS
8:00		
9:00		
10:00		
11:00		
12:00 PM		
1:00		
2:00		
3:00		
4:00		TO DO
5:00		
6:00		
7:00		
8:00		
9:00		
10:00		

breakfast	lunch	dinner

NOTES

water ○ ○ ○ ○ ○ ○ ○

exercise

SHARPEN THE SAW

In the book, Seven Habits of Highly Effective People by Stephen R. Covey; one of the seven habits to recall is sharpening the saw. One great way to sharpen the saw is to continue to build our skills and grow small habits into becoming a big thing in our lives.

I believe the key to self-improvement isn't to think bigger, but to think smaller. This means finding small habits that can build up exponentially over time.

There is a compounding effect of small habit changes and how positive behaviours can work together to have a great impact on your life. Therefore, giving this task a space in your journal will make a big impact.

This is a time to pause and make space in your life to remove the many unfinished ideas, dreams, goals, and repositioning them on paper. We then transform them to small habits; and track them. This is where we make a true action plan; and start nurturing it to become a big thing.

Let's have a short burst of science. Repair and improve your hippocampus. Automating behaviours in the form of habits is one of the best ways to do so. Your brain divides a complex pattern into small chunks. Each chunk is then automated, requiring less and less brain activity the more often it is repeated.

A new study from MIT neuroscientists has found that a small region of the brain's prefrontal cortex, where most thought and planning occurs, is responsible for moment-by-moment control of which habits are switched on at a given time.

"We've always thought — and I still do — that the value of a habit is you don't have to think about it. The journaling at this point becomes a power tool to help the plans and commitments that's required to help form this habit. Our pre-frontal cortex takes the opportunity to decide why it should remind you of the habit; if it realizes, you may not get comfort from it; it may not turn on the reminder. This does not happen with journaling your plans.

DAY 5

Sharpening the Saw. The most important tool for success journey is you! Yes, you. To be successful, the body speaks to us to ensure we are in the best shape. Today, commit to 3 small habits to take better care of yourself. Now is not the time to write the BIG HAIRY AUDACIOUS HABITS. These are the little ones. Instead of 30 mins exercise daily, commit to 4 mins. Instead of drinking 1 gallon of water daily, commit to 20 oz upon waking up. Instead of 6 to 8 hours sleep every night, commit to a special night. Instead of waking up 5am daily, choose 1 day.

#	Habit	Why
1		
2		
3		

Quote "Do not sacrifice long term happiness for short term gratification" D. Warren

Date:_____

I am grateful for:

7:00AM
8:00
9:00
10:00
11:00
12:00PM
1:00
2:00
3:00
4:00
5:00
6:00
7:00
8:00
9:00
10:00

GOALS

TO DO

breakfast	lunch	dinner

water ○ ○ ○ ○ ○ ○ ○ ○

NOTES

exercise

DECLUTTER

There is no need to journal this activity if you are truly clutter free in all aspects of your surroundings; however, if there are opportunities; create a space in your journal to tackle spaces and observe how it frees up your mind and the many other benefits.

Too much physical clutter impairs visual processing. It can be incredibly distracting to see lots of piles and disorganization in your surroundings, leading you to miss cues regarding people's emotions and other important information. Your cognition and clarity of mind are adversely affected by excess mental clutter.

Your journal is a place to be honest about your clutter and why it's there, allowing yourself to forgive and move on. From this empowered place, you can build towards the calm, peaceful living space you've always dreamed of.

To succeed in clearing clutter, you must keep promises to yourself and develop supportive habits. There are many other ways in which a journal helps to declutter your mind, often without any special effort. For one, journaling develops mindfulness — or slowing down and living in the moment — which makes for a clutter-free mind.

DAY 6

Making space. Life is filled with activities, sounds, things to do but beyond all that, there is a beautiful calming space that can be discovered when you make space for it. Today's activity is to declutter a space. Choose anywhere in the house, a junk drawer, 1 closet, car trunk, handbag, office desk. Just 1 space. Select the items you are not using. Categorize everything in 3 piles. Keep, Donate, And Discard. Everything you remove from the space you have freed up space for productivity. Now, make a list of everything you have in keep and donate categories. Create a permanent home for the items you are keeping.

ACTION	List Items
DONATE	
DISCARD	

Quote: "The more stuff you own, the more your stuff owns you."

Date:_____

I am grateful for:

7:00AM	
8:00	
9:00	
10:00	
11:00	
12:00PM	
1:00	
2:00	
3:00	
4:00	
5:00	
6:00	
7:00	
8:00	
9:00	
10:00	

GOALS

TO DO

breakfast

lunch

dinner

NOTES

water ◯ ◯ ◯ ◯ ◯ ◯ ◯ ◯

exercise

ADULT COLOURING

A few years ago during my art journeys, I came across adult colouring. I noticed it was becoming a thing; I did some research and went even further in realization that therapists use it as a method to help clients to **"take a pause".**

Don't you just love the science short bursts?! Colouring reduces stress and anxiety and has the ability to relax the fear center of your brain, the amygdala. It induces the same state as meditating by reducing the thoughts of a restless mind. This generates mindfulness and quietness, which allows your mind to get some rest after a long day at work.

It improves motor skills and vision. Colouring goes beyond being a fun activity for relaxation. It requires the two hemispheres of the brain to communicate. While logic helps us stay inside the lines, choosing colours generates a creative thought process.

We know we get a better night's sleep when avoiding engaging with electronics at night, because exposure to the emitted light reduces your levels of the sleep hormone, melatonin. Colouring is a relaxing and electronic-free bedtime ritual that won't disturb your level of melatonin.

Colouring requires you to focus, but not so much that it's stressful. It opens up your frontal lobe, which controls organizing and problem solving, and allows you to put everything else aside and live in the moment, generating focus.

You don't have to be an expert artist to colour! If you're looking for an uplifting way to unwind after a stressful day at work, colouring will surely do the trick. Pick something that you like and colour it however you like!

Enjoy the immediate benefits of colouring some days in your journal instead of writing.

DAY 7

Play with colours. Colours make us happy. It reminds us of the beauty life brings. It is even more beautiful when you let your imagination create a masterpiece.

Quotes "Every day may not be sweet. But there is something sweet in every day."

Date:_____

I am grateful for:

7:00 AM
8:00
9:00
10:00
11:00
12:00 PM
1:00
2:00
3:00
4:00
5:00
6:00
7:00
8:00
9:00
10:00

GOALS

TO DO

breakfast

lunch

dinner

NOTES

water ◯ ◯ ◯ ◯ ◯ ◯ ◯ ◯

exercise

GRATITUDE

If the only thing you do in your journal is being thankful! You are already on your way to a life of abundance. This is immediate benefit, embrace it. Just do it! Do it daily. Practicing gratitude creates a major shift in the mind that promotes a happier and more positive perspective that can be carried throughout the day.

Gratitude gives immediate benefit. A grateful person experiences a higher level of positive thoughts like love, happiness, and less stress level. When we practice gratitude in life, we are creating a happy and less competitive life around ourselves, therefore, the overall well-being of human beings increases.

Robert Emmons, a psychologist and world expert on gratitude defines gratitude as the ability to recognize the goodness in your life, which is due to your surroundings as well as the actions of another person or a group of people. Being grateful is a virtuous quality that allows you to not only see the best in other people but in your own life.

Also, gratitude improves feelings of hope and optimism, which allows you to more easily seek out positive solutions. When we focus on the negative, we see more negativity around us. Probably most significantly, research has shown that a regular gratitude practice can have physical benefits such as improved mood, better sleep and even reduce inflammation, to name a few.

Gratitude journaling can help you find out and focus on what really matters to you; keeping a gratitude journal helps you learn more about yourself and become more self-aware; your gratitude journal is for your eyes only, so you can write anything you feel. Just Do It. Now.

DAY 8

Gratitude. This may seem at first to be the most challenging, but when you start, you can't seem to stop. Write 50 things today to be thankful for.

Quote "Gratitude is the single most important ingredient to living a successful and fulfilled life." – Jack Canfield

Date:_____

I am grateful for:

7:00 AM
8:00
9:00
10:00
11:00
12:00 PM
1:00
2:00
3:00
4:00
5:00
6:00
7:00
8:00
9:00
10:00

GOALS

TO DO

breakfast	lunch	dinner

water ○ ○ ○ ○ ○ ○ ○ ○

NOTES

exercise

SELF-CARE

Self-care means taking all the steps you can to take care of your physical health and well-being, including hygiene, nutrition, managing stressor. Self-care is a broad term that encompasses just about anything you do to be good to yourself. In a nutshell, it's about being as kind to yourself as you would be to others.

To be intentional about self-care, we must build a plan to make it intentional and to achieve the goals and the end results of taking care of ourselves. Your journal is a perfect place to build a self-care plan. When it comes to self-care plans, there is no one-size-fits-all option. We all have different needs, strengths, and limitations.

The following are ideas of plans you can set in your journal to execute:

• Deep breathing

• Stretching

• Meditation

• Listening to music

• Exercising

• Reading

• Going for a walk

• Taking a spa-like bath or shower

• Socializing with friends

• Sitting outside and relaxing

• Engaging in a hobby

Before proceeding to building a self-care plan, begin by evaluating your current behaviours, schedules, and actions. Take a moment to consider what you value and need in your everyday life (daily self-care needs) versus what you value and need in the event of a crisis (emergency self-care needs).

It's a perfect way to thank your beautiful body! We know what happens when someone feels appreciated. Another immediate benefit to leverage.

DAY 9

Self-Care. You are reminded today of how special you are. You deserve a beautiful spa time shower. If you have a bath, go for it and prepare that bubble bath. No bath, that's fine. Shower will work. Let's plan for this. You will need your favourite candle, your best music playlist, your favourite body wash. Enjoy a beautiful, peaceful shower.

How was it? How did you plan the special spa time shower?

Quote: It's not selfish to love yourself, take care of yourself, and to make your happiness a priority.

Date:_____

I am grateful for:

7:00AM	**GOALS**
8:00	
9:00	
10:00	
11:00	
12:00PM	
1:00	
2:00	
3:00	
4:00	**TO DO**
5:00	
6:00	
7:00	
8:00	
9:00	
10:00	

breakfast	lunch	dinner

NOTES

water ◯ ◯ ◯ ◯ ◯ ◯ ◯

exercise

ACTION PLANNING

Journal automatically records actions that you choose which relate to specific situations and but making it purposeful is putting the actions in a Timeline view.

After few days of journaling, its recommended to take the time and benefit from what you have outlined. Make an action plan to help you launch the rocket on things that may need a kick-start.

SMART Action Planning - The SMART model was developed by psychologists as a tool to help people set and reach their goals.

S—Specific

 M—Measureable

A—Attainable

R—Realistic

T—Time-bound

Avoid setting unclear or vague objectives; instead be as precise as possible. We carry around many action plans in our brain daily, its time to create a routine in your journal to plan.

Action planning is the process of turning your strategy and goals into action. Taking your ideas and planning how to make them reality. In other words, action planning is working out what exactly you need to do to get where you want to be.

DAY 10

Take action! Awesome, you have been journaling. Today you will be making an action plan of Day 1 to 10. For each day's activity, you will write an action.

Action	Due By	Location	Status

Quote: Nothing happens until something moves.

Date:_____

I am grateful for:

	GOALS
7:00AM	
8:00	
9:00	
10:00	
11:00	
12:00PM	
1:00	
2:00	
3:00	

GOALS

4:00	**TO DO**
5:00	
6:00	
7:00	
8:00	
9:00	
10:00	

breakfast	lunch	dinner

NOTES

water ○ ○ ○ ○ ○ ○ ○ ○

exercise

MORNING ROUTINE

It is absolutely powerful to have a morning routine! Imagine waking up; and anything goes. Things may go well, until something that has no right in your morning activity comes in like an avalanche and starts to round things up, until one day it rolls over you. This may not be descriptive enough but, I just want to say; this is one of the areas in your life, where no one needs to plan for you. You are the Kings and Queens of the first 30 to 60 mins after waking up. Embrace this role in your life and use it, to take over the world. Use it to create the master plan, use it to simplify the rest of the day, use it control everything, use it to do what you always want to do.

Having a morning routine enables you to get more done while feeling less stress at the same time. When you start your day the same way every single day, you pick up momentum. Suddenly, you are making great progress on your big goals.

A morning routine is essentially a set of actions you perform in the morning, usually before starting your day's main activity like going to work or to school. The actions can be anything from drinking a glass of water or brushing your teeth to doing a two-hour workout or running around the block.

A morning routine takes the stress out of the start of the day and puts you on the best footing from the get-go. Of course, customize your morning routine for your own preferences.

Make it intentional, by telling your journal about your morning routine. Your journal believes in you, it doesn't judge, it doesn't erase, and it just cheers you on and believes in you.

DAY 11

Morning Routine. One of the most rewarding morning routines that keep me in check is making my bed. Oh yes! At first, I thought making breakfast was more rewarding but trying making your bed every day. Maybe you are already an expert at this, so today; take some time to write down a very simple morning routine. Even if you will not eventually stick to it, commit to this being the standard. Even if you deviate from your standard, you will adjust until it becomes a habit.

Time	Routine	Preparation Plan to win

Quote "The secret of your future is hidden in your daily routines."

Date:_____

I am grateful for:

7:00AM	**GOALS**
8:00	
9:00	
10:00	
11:00	
12:00PM	
1:00	
2:00	
3:00	**TO DO**
4:00	
5:00	
6:00	
7:00	
8:00	
9:00	
10:00	

breakfast	lunch	dinner

NOTES

water ○ ○ ○ ○ ○ ○ ○ ○

exercise

BUCKET LIST

Vacationing can have a profound effect on your physical and mental health and well-being – it's why we look forward to that time away! There are different types of vacations, though, and the adventure vacation lifestyle is growing in popularity for all the benefits it brings.

Now, get ready for a science rush!

The mental boost you get from adventure travel can be even more significant than the physical one. Visiting the Blue Mountain Peak and experiencing the view – with time to pause and reflect. Your everyday problems may seem insignificant compared with the bigger picture.

Being exposed to the new situations and cultures that travel brings about can also reboot your brain in ways you never thought possible. The daily cares that dominate your thoughts and sap your energy at home and work hold no sway when you're watching the water falling into the beautiful blue beaches!

With a steady supply of fresh air, your body will react positively. You'll have more energy, and your brain, which requires 20 percent of the oxygen you need, will function better. It's not just the air that makes a difference: in 2008, U.S. researchers found that spending time in a natural environment actually improves your focus and attention.

It won't happen on its own, and you will miss some beautiful places that come to mind form social media, conversations, newspapers, and TV and much more, if you don't create that space in your journal to magically outline your plan.

That list we make of our adventures and our travels can be titled in your journal as your bucket list.

DAY 12

Bucket List. Yes! Even writing it is rewarding. Today, make some time to think of all the great places you plan to visit locally and internationally. All the fun things you planned to do. Get a black and white version of your local map. Paste it here and place a red # at each location then list the location to represent each number below and the month or year you would like to complete it.

Paste Map Here:

List Places here

#	Activity or Place	Month / Year

"Let us step into the night and pursue that flighty temptress, adventure." — J.K. Rowling

Date:_____

I am grateful for:

7:00AM	
8:00	
9:00	**GOALS**
10:00	
11:00	
12:00PM	
1:00	
2:00	
3:00	
4:00	**TO DO**
5:00	
6:00	
7:00	
8:00	
9:00	
10:00	

breakfast	lunch	dinner

NOTES

water ◯ ◯ ◯ ◯ ◯ ◯ ◯ ◯

exercise

DAY 13

Colour and affirm. Spend some time today to colour. Choose the colours that make you happy. Imagine yourself stop resisting and start creating. Think about your creative side while doing this activity.

"Making a commitment to start" is one aspect of life. Actually "Starting" what you truly want to do in life is a completely different ball game."

DAY 14

Yay! You have completed day 14. You are just awesome. **Remind yourself daily. Life is beautiful and you have a purpose on this earth.** Make today great. Have a happy life. **Write a short message to your future self.**

Dear _____ (me, name), I am

_____.

CONCLUSION

Congratulations! You did it

In ending the 14 days, challenging ourselves to take action in using our journal purposefully, I would like to take this opportunity to thank you.

Remember, introspection is one of the most important human skills to master to become a more compassionate and overall better person.

A daily journal allows you to have that introspection — even if it's just a taste — to reflect on whom you were that day.

About the Author

Jamaica's aspiring bestselling author Debbie-Ann Warren.

Visit us on our private group 14daysjournalchallenges on Facebook.

Printed in Great Britain
by Amazon

84616542R00032